Words

A Fiction Writer's Guide
to
Serious Editing

Jane Riddell

By Jane Riddell

Second edition, published in 2016 by Jane Riddell

Cover Art: Krzysztof Kubik

Copyright © Jane Riddell

All Rights Reserved under the Copyright, Designs and Patents Act, 1988.

The moral right of the author has been asserted.

No part of this publication may be reproduced, copied, stored in a retrieval system, or transmitted, in any form or by any means, without the prior written consent of the copyright holder, nor be otherwise circulated in any form of binding or cover other than that in which it is published and without a similar condition being imposed on the subsequent purchaser.

Acknowledgements

Thanks to Gina Rossi, Anjana Chowdhury and Margaret Skea for their comprehensive feedback. In addition, I am grateful to the writers who have written such positive reviews of the first edition.

Contents

INTRODUCTION..1
METHOD...3
AT WHAT STAGE SHOULD YOU USE THE GUIDE?..6
THINGS TO CHECK: PART 1 - OVERVIEW EDITING..7
THINGS TO CHECK: PART 2 - LINE BY LINE EDITING 18
NEXT STEPS..48
RECOMMENDED BOOKS ON WRITING FICTION 49
ABOUT THE AUTHOR..51

INTRODUCTION

Writing a story or novel is relatively easy. Editing can be laborious. It's a bit like sculpting. You start with a slab of marble or wood and chisel away until you have a form you are happy with.

This guide is *not* a substitute for the myriad books about how to write. It therefore doesn't give detailed explanations about each of the aspects it covers. Rather, it provides a brief explanation of each one, a rationale for why it is important and, where appropriate, gives examples.

It is a suggested method for conducting a thorough check of what you have written, in a systematic and manageable way. You may not agree with some aspects of it. Editing, like writing, is a personal thing. Some of the best authors might ignore much of what is included. This guide won't compensate for a story that isn't worth telling or has many structural flaws. But if the basic craft is there, following this method will make your writing tighter, stronger and more readable: the best it can be.

The process is hard work, time consuming, requires concentration, perseverance and a tolerance of tedium, but when you reread a section after editing you will notice an improvement.

The guide is divided into two parts: the overview which addresses structural aspects, and the line-by-line editing section. Both are equally important. The structural points will contribute towards a cohesive, balanced piece of writing. Attention to the line-by-line section will result in readable and effective sentences.

Much of what follows is about balance: not over or under-explaining; conveying emotion without overdoing it; describing the setting without it dominating the story. It is also about ensuring that every sentence, phrase and word can justify its presence on the page.

While the approach is mechanical, it will enhance the creativity of the writing, rather than suppressing it. If there are techniques unfamiliar to you, try some of the recommended books on writing listed at the end of this guide.

Note: It is impossible for this guide to cover every aspect of writing that you might want to include in your checklist. You may think of many things to add as well as things you don't need to check. What is important is that you personalise the checklist to make it relevant and helpful for editing your own work.

METHOD

At this stage, you may be wondering whether or not you will manage to hold so much information in your head about the many aspects of writing which require editing. You may also wonder how you can check for so many things at the one time.

What works is to check a chapter, or the whole novel, for one aspect of writing at a time – for example, unnecessary adverbs. Using a table allows you to work your way through the list systematically, ticking as you go along. It means you don't have to remember what you've done and what you still have to do.

Furthermore, although there can be a logical order to checking, you don't need to stick to this. For example, if you are in the mood for eliminating extraneous words but not for checking for strong verb forms, this is okay. Once you've done this, you tick it off.

Overall, however, some aspects should ideally be checked after you have revised everything else; for example, there is little point in reading a chapter out loud for rhythm if you have still to check each sentence for clichés. Likewise, it would be a waste of time to delete unnecessary prepositions if you then proceed to discard an overly long chunk of character reflection.

An overview table can look something like this:

	Chapters	1	2	3	4	5	6	7
1	Appropriate pace	✓	✓	✓	✓	✓	✓	
2	Focus	✓	✓	✓	✓	✓	✓	✓
3	Scene has beginning, middle and end	✓	✓	✓	✓	✓	✓	
4	Scene beginning with action	✓	✓	✓	✓	✓	✓	
5	Plot or character revealed	✓	✓	✓	✓	✓	✓	✓
6	Character interaction	✓	✓	✓	✓	✓	✓	

A line-by-line table could look like this:

Chapters		1	2	3	4	5	6	7
1	Minimal use of passive voice	✓	✓	✓	✓	✓		
2	No showing then telling	✓	✓	✓	✓	✓		
3	No overwriting	✓	✓	✓	✓			
4	Minimal use of names in dialogue	✓	✓	✓	✓	✓		
5	Use of beats	✓	✓	✓	✓	✓		
6	Dialogue purpose (no info dumping)	✓	✓	✓				
7	Use of subtext	✓	✓	✓	✓	✓		

Note: There may be other techniques you want to include in either your overview or line-by-line checklists.

AT WHAT STAGE SHOULD YOU USE THE GUIDE?

If you have recently completed the first draft of your novel and anticipate some serious rewriting – for example, removing scenes/chapters, axing a character, changing the ending, switching from third person narrative to first person – then it's advisable to undertake these changes before editing. There is no point in vigorously checking a piece of text which you might subsequently delete. Once you are satisfied with the story overall, then it is time to do some overview and line-by-line editing.

For the same reason, it makes sense to conduct the overview editing before the line-by-line.

You might think about whether or not to embark on this editing process before or after giving your story to a reader for comment. This depends on what sort of feedback you are seeking. If you want an opinion on whether the story works overall, then approaching a reader before you have done a comprehensive edit would be more logical, as their feedback might result in your making significant structural changes. At the same time, a thoroughly edited text is more likely to result in a positive response.

THINGS TO CHECK: PART 1 - OVERVIEW EDITING

Hooking the reader with the opening line

Some readers may give the book several pages to whet their interest. Others will not. Lovers of literary fiction are more likely to tolerate descriptive passages before the protagonist first appears.

Appropriate pace

It is important not to rush from one piece of action to the next. Characters need time to reflect on what has just happened. Readers want to know their reactions. Be particularly careful about not rushing significant parts.

Focus

Are you hopping from one storyline to another, or is it clear what the scene/chapter is about?

Scene beginning with action

Beginning a scene with action is more likely to hook the reader than beginning with reflection or description, although this depends on genre. A "quieter" novel will have more reflection than an action story. Note that in this context dialogue counts as action. Ideally every scene should be joined (in the writer's head) by the word 'but' or 'however', meaning that the story is driving forward.

Scene ending with action

It's important to make sure your scene has an ending and doesn't just stop, to avoid the reader becoming confused. The exception to this is the cliffhanger.

Do you have a closing line that will urge the reader to continue reading?

Plot or characterisation building to conclusion

Scenes/chapters must drive the plot or reveal more about the personality of one of the key characters, in other words, have purpose. If your scene builds to a conclusion, you will know it achieves a purpose and isn't simply padding.

Character interaction

Do characters interact with each other rather than spending large chunks of time in solitary reflection? Over-reflection slows down the pace. However, the proportion of reflection compared with action will vary depending on the type of writing. A literary author such as Anita Brookner may have page after page of introspection. Someone writing a comic romp will include little soul-searching.

No excessive foreshadowing

While it's important to set the stage for what happens, so that when it does, it seems plausible, guard against making it too easy for the reader to guess what lies ahead.

Smooth scene transitions, located in time

To prevent the reader getting lost, scene transitions

must identify place, time, and viewpoint character (where there are multiple viewpoints), especially if there's been a change in any of the three. Scene transitions can be as short as two words – *That night…* – or as long as several paragraphs. If they are too long, they become information dumps and/or long stretches of telling instead of showing.

Links between scenes or chapters can be helpful – for example where the weather is significant in one scene, the next scene could begin with 'The following day the wind was even stronger so we abandoned our idea of going for a walk.' This both signals the setting change and links the chapters.

Ways to locate the reader in time:

- The leaves were yellowing…
- On a cold spring morning…
- Giles sat at his kitchen table as a slow twilight descended over Banchory.
- A month after her arrival, Sienna…
- After an hour had passed, Sophie realised he wouldn't turn up.
- From her study window she watched him weeding in the afternoon heat.
- Fraser lay on the trampoline staring at the stars.
- Snow fell on the mountains around Brunnen.
- Halfway through dinner, Graham felt sick.

♦ For the third time that week, she breakfasted alone.

Mix of action and static scenes and summary

Stories need variety. Too much drama and the story becomes melodramatic and implausible. Too many static scenes (descriptive or reflecting a character's thoughts) and the reading is dull. Some actions only justify summarising. Again the balance of action and reflection depends on the style of your writing. Have you achieved the balance that is appropriate for your story?

Avoiding melodrama

Melodrama occurs when the writer tries too hard to make the reader feel sympathy for the character, resulting in a different response. Action and dialogue should convey the tragedy, especially when fresh images are used, rather than clichés.

It's often the exact opposite of melodrama – what characters are *not* doing – that conveys the most powerful emotions.

For example, when lovers gaze into each other's eyes, we all know what that means. But what if one of them looks away or won't meet the eyes of the other? What if they say goodbye and one doesn't wave, or look back? Less is more. Doing nothing can be powerful.

Additionally, having banal things going on simultaneously can heighten tension. For example, when someone is handed a letter or receives a phone call with shocking news, this comes over more powerfully if around her the waiter is still serving lunch, or the concert is about to start, or he is paying for a shirt in a shop.

Conveying mood or tension

Conveying tension is a large part of what keeps the reader reading. One of the easiest ways to create tension is through dialogue. See section on subtext.

Providing breaks from tension

Readers, like writers, need respites where they can relax for a while. During these parts, characters may be involved with mundane tasks, for example planting seedlings, hanging a picture. Tense sections will have more impact if they are interspersed with lower key writing. Have you included some breaks from tension?

Note: Try to avoid some of the more clichéd activities such as taking a shower, making coffee.

Including happy passages

These are important to avoid the tone of the story being too downbeat. Misery memoirs only work if there are occasional let-ups from unhappiness.

These could be as simple as pleasure derived from listening to music, eating chocolate or receiving an unexpected compliment.

Rooted in the present

Is your scene/chapter rooted in the present? Whilst references to something in the past can explain something or provide a usual backdrop, if there is too much of this, then the reader feels as though they are taken out of the story. This doesn't apply to novels which contain double plots, that is, switching between past and present, telling two narratives.

Mix of narrative closeness and distance, and panning out

Have you included a mix of narrative closeness and distance?

Just as a film has a mixture of narrative distance, so should a story. If there is too much narrative closeness, where the reader is sitting on the character's shoulder, this can become claustrophobic.

Likewise, when readers aren't privy to what a character thinks, they can feel detached from that character and unengaged. A panning-out shot – where figures shrink as they walk away along the beach, or gaze at distant mountains - is also important for variety.

Narrative distance

- ♦ The reader sees things as they really happen.
- ♦ The narrator relays the story in a neutral voice, occasionally letting the reader see into the mind of the viewpoint character. The thoughts are told, rather than shown, because of the use of taglines (he said/she asked).

Narrative closeness

- ♦ The reader sees things not as they really happen, but as the character thinks they happen.

- ♦ The narrator is more inside the character, showing the thoughts, rather than outside the character, telling the thoughts. As the thoughts are in the character's mind, there aren't any taglines.

Examples:

Narrative distance

Claire sat at her desk, every muscle in her body tense from anger. <u>She allowed herself a moment of self-pity, her usual failing</u>. Other people had understanding bosses, <u>she thought</u>. Jenni's, for instance, let her take an extended lunch break when her boyfriend was in hospital. <u>She wished</u> her boss was like that.

The underlined parts show narrative distance. The reader isn't allowed to be so close to the character.

Narrative closeness

Claire sat at her desk, every muscle in her body tense from anger. Other people had understanding bosses. Jenni, for instance – her boss let her take an extended lunch break when her boyfriend was in hospital. Why couldn't Claire have a boss like that? It wasn't fair.

Panning out

She watched the couple walk away, their figures gradually shrinking, rendered insignificant as the sky blushed with pink and gold.

Panning in and out
Examples:

> In the distance, mountains were hazy in the midday sun. The hotel gardens were empty of guests.

> Debbie knocked on the side door again but no one replied. She was sure the interview was today. She checked her diary for the third time: Thursday, April 4: Castle Hotel, 12 noon. Take CV.

The above is an example of a camera panning in from the surroundings to an anxious character checking her diary.

Providing the right amount of explanation

While you don't want the reader to be confused, over-explanation can appear cloying and irritating. Give the readers enough information but leave them space to work things out for themselves. An example of this is when a piece of dialogue fails to convey what it aims to and the writer then explains what that was.

Example:

> 'You don't need to walk me to school, Mum,' Mary said. She didn't want embarrassing Mum walking her to the school gates.

is more clearly understood by:

> 'Mum, don't walk me to school. None of the other parents do that,' Mary said.

In the second example, the dialogue conveys Mary's embarrassment at her mother walking her to school.

No explanatory sentence is required.

Characters changing

Central characters should change but this can be in a subtle way: for example, being in possession of a new piece of knowledge, having a sudden insight or a shift in attitude.

Have you checked for indications of your characters changing?

Physical/cerebral embodiment

To empathise or even engage with a character, the reader needs to know how that character thinks, and how he/she feels, both physically and emotionally. Does a character always develop a migraine after she's had lunch with her mother? Does the sound of the sea make someone yearn for their childhood or be glad they have left home?

Subtle conveying of emotion

Underplay rather than over-sentimentalise.

There is a saying which goes: *If the character cries, the reader won't*. Describing the body language of the character can be more powerful than saying 'she felt weighed down with grief'. American author, Anita Shreve, is highly skilled at conveying strong emotions.

The following example is taken from her novel, *Light on Snow*, a story narrated by a twelve-year-old girl who has recently lost her mother and baby brother in a road traffic accident.

>One day, several weeks after the accident, I came

home from school on the bus and found my father sitting in the same chair in which I'd left him at breakfast, a wooden chair next to the kitchen table. I was sure that the cup of coffee on the table, with its dark sludge on the bottom, was the same one he'd poured himself at 8 am.

This is a more subtle communication of immeasurable grief than had the author written:

When I arrived home from school, I found my father sobbing his heart out at the kitchen table.

Setting/description interwoven and working

Although description helps the reader visualise the story, too much can read like a travelogue. Make it clear how the character is reacting to their environment, either positively or negatively. Such description should serve at least one of the following:

- give information about time and place
- set a mood
- suggest character – how they react to where they are
- place characters in the socioeconomic spectrum
- convey attitudes of characters – including suggesting something that will happen

Example:

Everywhere she looked on the beach, she saw couples: linking arms, sharing a cigarette, kissing, unpacking a picnic. She walked home.

Including sensual details

Have you deployed all the senses, not just sight? Smells, sounds, what something feels like when touched, how food tastes, help enrich the story and allow the reader to feel they are experiencing the action, especially when unusual details are included.

Weaving

Avoid 'slab' writing. Interweave action, dialogue and reflection. In real life our day isn't divided into chunks of doing, talking and thinking. These will be mixed together. When reflecting, avoid repeating thoughts. Although we do this in real life, this can become boring on the page.

Deleting unnecessary domestic bits

Do you have too many scenes about meals, squabbling children or unruly pets? Housework? Paying the bills?

Making it clear what is going on

With each main scene, the following should be clear:

- ♦ What the point of view character wants
- ♦ What happens /goes wrong
- ♦ Why it matters

Answering the reader's questions

Have you tied up all the loose ends? Have the subplots been resolved or at least addressed?

THINGS TO CHECK: PART 2 - LINE BY LINE EDITING

No showing then telling

If you have shown something, you don't then need to tell the reader what you've shown. This is a form of over-explaining. Please refer to the earlier section on providing the right amount of explanation.

Example:

> Andy was furious. He threw a candle across the sitting room.

The reader knows that Andy was furious by the act of throwing the candle.

Overwriting

Have you checked for overwriting? Sometimes it's possible to end a paragraph with an earlier sentence. Less is more.

Example:

> The doctor advised me to take you to hospital immediately. You were eighteen months old. <u>Fear gripped me.</u>

The underlined sentence is superfluous. Any parent would be frightened. It is enough to mention the child's age. The reader will empathise.

Avoiding overuse of names in dialogue

This can be irritating. It can also take the reader out

of the story. An exception is where it is a personality trait of a character, or where you want to make it clear who is speaking without using a tagline.

Example:

'I thought you'd be pleased, Maggie.'

'I am pleased, John. I'm just not keen about the timing.'

'Well, Maggie. Let me know when the timing is right.'

'Okay, John. I will.'

Using beats

Beats are descriptions of physical action, interspersed in dialogue.

They have many functions, including avoiding the need for overuse of 'he said', 'she asked', and making it easier for the reader to imagine the scene.

Balance is important. Too many beats can be perceived as an irritating interruption and as limiting the reader's imagination. Too few of them and the dialogue becomes disorientating. When you want to increase tension, reduce the beats to a minimum. Beats should be varied and fresh.

Example:

As Sienna helped Philippe out of bed, Odette appeared, her hair mussed from sleep.

'What's wrong with Philippe?' she asked.

'He has an infection,' Sienna said.

'Is he going to die?' Odette asked.

'No! But he needs medicine. You should go back to bed,' Sienna said.

'I want to help. I could phone Mama,' Odette said.

reads better as:

As Sienna helped the child out of bed, Odette appeared, her hair mussed from sleep.

'What's wrong with Philippe?'

'He has an infection.'

'Is he going to die?'

Sienna forced herself to sound calm. 'No. But he needs medicine. You should go back to bed.'

Odette yawned. 'I want to help. I could phone Mama.'

Checking for a purpose in dialogue

Dialogue should move the story on or reveal character. It shouldn't be used to dump information on the reader.

Example:

'You remember that holiday we had as kids, just before Mum and Dad told us they were getting a divorce and we'd be living with Dad from now on – just before I broke my leg and spent three weeks in hospital…'

Avoid repeating what the reader already knows unless it is a major event. For example, if the heroine is late for an exam because she stopped to help someone who had been knocked off her bike, just have her hand over the verification statement from the police and ask when she can take the exam again.

This avoids getting into a one-step-forward-one-step-back situation.

Using subtext in dialogue

Have you included subtext in your dialogue? Real people don't always state what they actually mean or feel, because there's too much at stake. Instead they talk around a subject, with humour, distraction, outright denial, etc.

When a character states exactly what he wants it's called on-the-nose (OTN) dialogue. There's no hidden meaning behind the words, because everything is spelled out.

Subtext is what characters are really talking about beneath what they appear to be talking about. Under dialogue there can be conflict, anger, competition, pride, showing off, or other implicit ideas and emotions.

Subtext lends emotional and intellectual depth, allowing the reader to feel first and understand second. Without it the novel will begin to feel repetitive and tedious, the characters implausible.

Types of subtext

- ♦ Using action as a response: If one character makes an offensive comment to another character, the other might walk out of the room.

- Changing the subject/misdirection: Have the character evade a direct response.
- Using words or phrases that have a double meaning.
- Answering a question with a question: This technique is often used when a character has something to hide.
- Deliberate lying
- Lying by omission
- Non-sequitur answer: This is where the response doesn't connect with the original comment. Unlike changing the subject or misdirection, it isn't necessarily a deliberate attempt to avoid replying to the comment.
- Use of satire (irony, sarcasm)
- Feigning politeness or another emotion
- Silence

Example:

Alison arrives home late after work. Peter is upset because he has cooked a special meal.

Peter: Where were you?

Alison: I was shopping.

Peter: Why?

Alison: I realised I had nothing smart to wear to your brother's wedding.

Peter: Why didn't you let me know you'd be late?

I cooked something special.

Alison: I wish you'd told me you were doing that. But you're right. I should have texted you. I'll do that next time.

Peter: Please do. If I'd known what time you'd be back, I'd have put the meat on later. Did you buy something?

Alison: Yes, as it happens, I did. Do you want to see it?

Peter: Yes. I'll just reheat the veg. Why don't you put on the dress or whatever it is?

Alison: Okay, be back in a mo. What have you cooked?

Peter: Stroganoff, your favourite. Then rhubarb crumble.

Alison: I knew I was right to settle with a guy who enjoys cooking.

This OTN dialogue does nothing to intrigue the reader. Everything is spelled out.

Using subtext, the previous conversation might read like this:

Peter: Where were you?

Alison: Why do you worry so much? **(question responded to by another question)**

Peter: I had a lovely meal ready. Now it's ruined.

Alison: If you had me on a lead, you'd still worry about where I was. **(changing the subject)**

Peter: I read somewhere that couples are more likely to stray if they never check on what the other's up to.

Alison: Something you found on Twitter? **(sarcasm)**

Silence (silence)

Alison: If you really, simply can't bear not knowing **(sarcasm)**, I was buying a dress for your brother's wedding. The assistant said I looked good in it.

Peter: Where is it, then?

Alison: Where's what? **(question responded to by another question)**

Peter: This sexy dress you bought. **(sarcasm)**

Alison: I'm starving. What did you cook? **(question responded to by another question, changing the subject)**

Peter storms out of the flat. **(responding with action)**

The second piece of dialogue suggests several things about this couple. Peter is insecure in his relationship and Alison is fed up with such insecurity. She enjoys tormenting him. She also looks down on him intellectually. He has a temper. The scene has subtext.

Including dialogue on most pages

This brings life to your writing. Avoid long pieces of exposition or reflection. As mentioned earlier, if you are writing a literary novel, there will be more introspection than will be found in a commercial story.

Using punctuation to increase impact of narrative and dialogue

This can be a good way of conveying someone under stress. Ellipses, commas, colons and semicolons all have a role to play. Listen to films and study how words are grouped together. A good example of this is spoken by Molly, the heroine in the film *Falling in Love:*

> I don't know – he looked nice…. He looked sort of familiar.
>
> Except, you know, for a minute I thought…. I thought…. It was really nothing. And I just, you know…. Something.
>
> It's just a little funny story, that's all. I mean, Jesus, I'm really sorry I mentioned it. Let's just forget it. Okay?

Avoiding clichés

Have you removed any clichés? Tired expressions give writing a jaded feel. Go for fresh language, but don't overdo it. Whilst using a thesaurus can be helpful, avoid using words that you aren't familiar with or that result in a change of register. (Please refer to next section.) If you google clichés you will find lists of them!

Example:

> It seemed to take forever for Helen to say goodbye to the friends she'd made on holiday.

reads more freshly as:

> By the time Helen had said goodbye to the friends

she'd made on holiday, climate change had been sorted.

Note: An exception is when tired language is a personality trait of one of your characters. There are people who speak in clichés. Be careful, however, not to overdo this characteristic.

Avoiding a change of register

Avoid having a change of register, that is, a character who normally talks or thinks in plain language suddenly using a more sophisticated word, unless that character is making a point, for example, trying to impress.

Example:

I was walking along the road, looking at the posh houses and poncy cars, wondering if I'd ever be able to afford even a secondhand bike. *(change of rcegister)* But material possessions are just an illusion of wealth, aren't they? It's the spiritual things that count.

Have you checked for any changes of register?

Making the most of sentences

A sentence can be grammatical but functionally weak. The following information will help to strengthen sentences.

Specific language

Avoid using verb phrases containing nouns when a verb or noun on its own will suffice. For example, instead of writing 'People waiting to see the doctor' simply use the word 'patients'.

Avoid turning good action words into nouns.

Example:

In the car, she gave him directions to the restaurant.

reads better as:

In the car she directed him to the restaurant.

Note: An exception might be when you wish to be emphatic.

Example:

When Liz phoned the following evening, Sienna described Philippe's illness.

is less emphatic than:

When Liz phoned the following evening, Sienna launched into a description of Philippe's illness.

Verb choice

Choose strong, descriptive verbs that can be visualised and add impact.

Example:

The woman walked quickly into the town hall and asked to speak to the person in charge.

reads better as:

The woman marched into the town hall and demanded to speak to the person in charge.

Have you checked to see if any weak verbs can be replaced by more precise ones?

Selecting strong verb forms: active voice rather than passive

Using the active voice as much as possible adds energy to your writing. It allows the reader to be in the middle of the action, whereas the passive voice makes her a spectator. Many novels are ruined by overuse of the passive voice.

Example:

> The factory was destroyed by the fire.

reads better as:

> The fire destroyed the factory.

Strong tenses

Guard against overuse of the pluperfect: had eaten, had read. Too many of these slow down the pace and give the text a laborious feel.

Example:

> James <u>had</u> arrived late, <u>had</u> adjusted the metal coathanger which served as an aerial for his Citröen and <u>had</u> given her his customary peck, missing her mouth. When he <u>had</u> left early, claiming a headache – from her incense, of course, not his smoking (nothing that happened to James was ever his fault) – she <u>had</u> been relieved as she <u>had</u> needed her bed for herself.

> *(six uses of pluperfect)*

reads better as:

> James <u>had</u> arrived late, adjusted the metal coat hanger which served as an aerial for his Citröen and given her his customary peck, missing her mouth. When he left early, claiming a headache – from her incense, of course, not his smoking (nothing that happened to James was ever his fault) – <u>she'd</u> been relieved, needing her bed for herself.

> *(two uses of pluperfect, one in contracted form)*

Positioning of clauses

Placing the main verb near the beginning or the end of sentences generates emphasis. If your sentence has several subordinate clauses, position the main clause at the end so that it is visible and the sentence is clear.

Example:

> The curtain comes down as soon as the actors have taken their last bow.

reads better as:

> As soon as the actors have taken their last bow, down comes the curtain.

If the main verb isn't placed in a clear and obvious position, a longer sentence won't be so effective.

Example:

> He headed straight for the hotel after he left work because he was exhausted from being up so early and needed to be fresh for the following day.

reads better as:

> Exhausted from being up so early and needing to be fresh for the following day, after work he headed straight for the hotel.

In the second example, the main clause is clear because it is placed at the end of a long sentence.

Varied sentence constructions

Avoid monotony by using different sentence structures within a paragraph, including sentence beginnings.

Ensure that you don't have too many sentences starting with 'he' or 'she' next to each other. Do you start too many sentences with 'as'? If so, replace some of these with 'when' or 'while'.

Example:

> She eventually removed her damp coat and ran a bath. She lit two rose-scented candles, added energising bath lotion, and lowered her body into the water. She felt cosy, safe in the dark blue walls of the tiny bathroom. Her feet made little waves with the bubbly water, she disappeared under it, savouring its warmth. She surfaced, soaped herself, and turned on the radio.

reads better as:

> Eventually she removed her damp coat and ran a bath. She lit two rose-scented candles, added energising bath lotion, and lowered her body into the water. The dark blue walls of the tiny bathroom felt cosy, safe, like returning to the womb. Her feet made little waves with the bubbly

water, she disappeared under it, savouring its warmth. She surfaced, soaped herself, and turned on the radio.

Sometimes all that's required to vary sentence openings is to remove the character's name or pronoun.

Example:

She remembers Dorothy reading to her from the crimson armchair. She recalls the various family crises during her formative years, the knowledge she was always welcome here.

reads better as:

She remembers Dorothy reading to her from the crimson armchair. Recalls the various family crises during her formative years, the knowledge she was always welcome here.

Here are some ways of beginning sentences.

- ♦ There is… Here…
- ♦ Use a verb with -ed or an -ed clause

Example:

Moved beyond words, she watched the sun rise over the desert.

Use a simile

Example:

Like a butcher, she hacked her way through a French sentence.

Use an adverb

Examples:

Abruptly, she got up and left the table.

Likewise, his son could be vicious.

Use a preposition

Above, across, after, at, before, behind, below, beneath, beside, between, by, down, for, from, inside, in, near, of, off, over, through, to, towards, under, up, with.

Examples:

In the distance, the snow-covered Atlas mountains beckoned.

Beneath her, on a flat concrete roof, two scrawny cats stretched in the midday sun.

Use a connective

Examples:

While I read to the children, Mike did the washing up.

Meanwhile, there was work to be done.

Use a conjunction, for example, 'but', 'and'

Examples:

But then she saw the policeman heading straight for her.

And now she knew Tom wasn't coming back, it was easier to decide what to do.

Note: Starting a sentence with 'but' can be a useful way of increasing pace, but this shouldn't be used too often.

Note: An exception to the principle of varying sentence beginnings is when you want to create a certain effect or a specific rhythm, for impact.

Example:

> Richie calls, arranges to come for dinner. He arrives, tired, his jacket crushed, a brown stain on his cord trousers. He flops into a chair, lifts the paper. He switches on the television, watches a news programme, changes to golf, then to a soap, his expression vacant. He wanders round the sitting room, peering out of windows, lifting plants and examining the soil for dryness.

In the above paragraph, the writer deliberately starts four successive sentences with 'he' to convey a negative mood.

Sentence length

Varying sentence length prevents monotonous reading. Several long sentences can be followed by a short one, or even a sentence fragment, such as 'If only', and 'Worth a try'. Sentence fragments should be used sparingly.

Sentence length can also be used for controlling pace. In general, short sentences are more dramatic and therefore increase pace.

Long sentences can either increase or slow down pace, depending on how they are written. The following techniques increase the pace of a long sentence:

- ♦ Omitting descriptions, adjectives etc.
- ♦ Using strong, precise verbs
- ♦ Using simple, obvious words as these are easy to read
- ♦ Joining two short sentences with 'and'.

Conversely, including description and several clauses can slow down the pace of a long sentence.

Example of slower pace:

> The first impression I had when I arrived early at the beautiful, old stone building, the family home of the Andrews children, was of resigned chaos, as the mother, a prematurely grey-haired woman, gathered muddy trainers and sweatshirts from what I assumed to be the schoolroom, a large, airy space with a round table, then asked the youngest child, a scrawny boy with a blotchy skin, to please go and find Lizzy.

Example of faster pace:

> When I arrived early at the Andrews' family home, it was chaotic, the mother, rushing around scooping up shoes and sweatshirts from the schoolroom, and asking the youngest boy to clean the whiteboard and pleading with another boy to go and find Lizzy.

As already mentioned, shorter sentences convey pace. Sentences joined by commas also evoke urgency and increase pace. However, overly paced writing can have a staccato effect. Read your text out loud to see if you have overdone the short sentences.

Punctuation for effective sentences

This is a personal thing. There are few rigid rules.

Commas should be used to aid clarity and allow a break between words. They can also increase pace and strengthen a sentence, by replacing 'and'.

Example:

Power is addictive and dangerous and all-consuming.

reads better as:

Power is addictive, dangerous, all-consuming.

Note: Be careful before adding commas which take the reader out of the present action. Excessive use of commas can metaphorically trip up the reader.

Colons can be used to emphasise key words.

Example:

I believe that he will reach the top and not merely do well.

reads better as:

I believe that he won't merely do well: he will reach the top.

Exclamation marks are visually distracting and, if overused, are irritating. They should be reserved for moments when a character is physically shouting or experiencing the mental equivalent. When used frequently, it looks as if you are trying to infuse your dialogue or narration with excitement.

Using liposuctioning (term invented for this context by Sol Stein)

This is about eliminating any words which don't earn their keep. Superfluous words and phrases slow the pace and weaken impact and the reader's attention. You may be surprised by how many of these you can delete in one chapter.

Wherever possible, avoid using adverbs to describe verbs

Much of the time there should be a strong and precise enough verb available, which will render an adverb redundant.

Example:

He walked with purpose along the road.

reads better as:

He strode along the road.

If no active verb exists, then include an adverb.

Note: If you are using adverbs, positioning them after the verb results in a stronger sentence.

Example:

She strolled into the gallery and aimlessly looked around.

reads better as:

> She wandered into the gallery and looked around aimlessly.

Delete unnecessary adjectives

For each adjective, ask yourself if it is an important part of a description.

Check for unnecessary verbs

Example:

> It was also the day Véronique was coming to collect Philippe.

reads more succinctly as:

> It was also the day Véronique was collecting Philippe.

Example:

> I'm going to have to go to the gym.

reads more succinctly as:

> I'll have to go to the gym.

Note: Using the phrase 'going to have to...' instead of 'have to...' is often found in writing and is clunky(!)

The verbs 'prepare,' 'decide,' 'start,' 'begin,' 'attempt' are often, but not always, redundant.

Example:

He began to laugh

reads better as:

He laughed.

There is no such thing as beginning to laugh. Once you have started, you are laughing (!)

Example:

He decided to confront his neighbour.

reads more strongly as:

He confronted his neighbour.

Tighten prepositional phrases

Example:

The iPad of my friend

reads better as:

my friend's iPad.

Reduce prepositions

Words such as 'in,' 'for,' 'at,' 'on,' 'through,' and 'over' can make a sentence clunky and unclear.

Example:

The reason for the failure of the hockey team of the University of York in the final game against the team from the University of Edinburgh was that on that day and at that time some of the players were recovering from a wild party the night before. (48 words) *reads better as:*

> York University's hockey team lost the final game against Edinburgh University because some of its players were recovering from a wild party the night before. (25 words)

Reconstruction results in a clearer sentence with almost half the number of words.

The prepositions 'up' and 'down' can often be eliminated.

Example:

> He lifted up his head

reads better as:

> He lifted his head.

Remove all redundant relative pronouns and auxiliary or linking verbs

Example:

> Laws <u>which</u> are too rigid and counterproductive

reads better as:

> Laws too rigid and counterproductive

Check for unnecessary usage of 'because'

Things don't need to be explained; they need to be stated.

Example:

> I went to the dentist because I needed a check-up.

reads better as:

I went to the dentist for a check-up.

Omit unnecessary indefinite articles 'a,' 'an' and 'one'

Example:

The world is a complex one.

reads better as:

The world is complex.

Omit unnecessary definite articles ('the')

Example:

The waves crashed onto the shore.

reads better as:

Waves crashed onto the shore.

The following words frequently (but not always) constitute flab:

however

though

almost

entire

successive

respective

perhaps

always

somehow

that (particularly if following a noun)

just

only

still

well

of course

Note: The exception is when such words are characteristic of a person's speech pattern. Sometimes rhythm dictates that you add one of these words to ensure a smoother flow between sentences.

Delete redundant pairs

First and foremost

Each and every

Hopes and dreams

Full and complete

Always and forever

Example:

For each and every shirt you purchase, you will receive a free tie.

reads better as:

For every shirt you purchase, you will receive a free tie.

Delete unnecessary qualifiers

really

basically

probably

very

definitely

somewhat

kind of

extremely

practically

Example:

Because a great many of my clothes are basically things I would no longer wear, it would really be a very good idea to give some of them away to charity. (31 words)

reads more succinctly as:

Because I no longer wear many of my clothes, I should give some of them away to charity. (18 words)

Delete unnecessary modifiers

A modifier is an optional word or phrase which changes or adds to the meaning of a sentence.

Normally the modifier can be removed without making the sentence ungrammatical.

Example:

The airport is usually busy.

is still grammatical with the modifier removed:

> The airport is busy.

Sometimes such modifiers are unnecessary because the intended meaning can be conveyed without adding them.

Examples:

> Do not anticipate in advance that you will fail all your exams.

reads better as:

> Do not anticipate that you will fail all your exams.

In the above example, 'anticipate' already implies that something is in advance.

> I will try to collect you as soon as possible.

reads better as:

> I will collect you as soon as possible.

In the example above, including both 'try to' and 'as soon as possible' is unnecessary, as both these convey the same intention: doing something quickly.

Replace a phrase with a word

Many commonly used phrases which detract from meaning can be replaced with single words. These include:

> the reason for
>
> due to the fact that
>
> in light of the fact that
>
> given the fact that

and considering the fact.

All the above can be replaced with 'because', 'since' or 'why'.

Example:

In light of the fact that I've been feeling tired, I'm going away for the weekend.

reads more succinctly as:

Since I've been feeling tired, I'm going away for the weekend.

Conditional phrases

In the event that…

Under circumstances in which…

Both the above can be replaced with 'if'.

Example:

In the event that the fire alarm goes off, you should make your way outside by the stairs.

reads more succinctly as:

If the fire alarm goes off, you should make your way outside by the stairs.

The phrases*:*

It is necessary that

Cannot be avoided

can be replaced with 'must' or 'should'.

Example:

It is necessary that he sees the doctor to have his

medicine changed.

reads more succinctly as:

He must see the doctor to have his medicine changed.

Time phrases

Example:

At this moment in time

This can be replaced by 'now'.

Note: The above 'wordy' expressions/phrases could be justified if they are used to convey the way a character talks.

Become aware of pet words or phrases that infiltrate your writing too often. Excessive use of these can be checked out by using the 'find' facility on a computer.

Note: It might be helpful to create a table for extraneous words you have a tendency to use.

Variety of voices

To distinguish characters from each other, vary their speech patterns and vocabulary, their sentence lengths, their degree of articulation, their ability to listen or need to interrupt. Diction refers to tone and style of sentences. There are high, medium and low levels of diction:

Example:

I'd went oot 'cos ma mither and faither were at each other's throats.　　　　(low level)

I'd gone out because my mum and dad were arguing. (ordinary level)

I went to the cinema to avoid witnessing yet another altercation between my parents. (high level)

Paragraph length

Avoid overly long paragraphs. Readers want to see some white space on the page. Short paragraphs increase pace; one-sentence paragraphs increase emphasis. It's also a good idea to introduce a new idea by a new paragraph.

Formatting

Have you checked for correct indenting, speech marks and full stops? Each new paragraph should be indented, except for the first paragraph of each new section of text, or point of view change. Leave breaks to indicate a new location or passage of time.

Rhythm

Reading a chapter out loud is the easiest way of determining if your text flows – when you want it to. Overuse of a person's name when starting sentences not only can sound irritating, it also spoils the rhythm. Overuse of the pronoun 'he' or 'she' to replace the name can be confusing, especially in a conversation. As well as guarding against using names too much, *where* they are used can affect whether the text reads smoothly or jars.

Including a mixture of long and short sentences helps achieve a good rhythm, as well as affecting pace. The rhythm you want to achieve will depend to some extent on the type of novel you have written. A more literary story which is driven by character and mood, will tend to deploy long, descriptive sentences, whereas an action story will opt for shorter sentences to achieve a faster pace.

Note: Reading your work out loud to check its rhythm is more effective than reading it silently. Only when you hear the words will you be able to improve the rhythm.

NEXT STEPS

Having read through the above, now devise your own editing table(s). Make a note of all the items you think should be checked. Add anything else which hasn't been included.

The table should be as relevant/personal to your writing as possible. You may be aware of a tendency to include too many bouts of illness, meals eaten etc. These can be added to your checklist. In the liposuctioning section (for which you may want to devise a separate table), you may be aware of certain words which creep into your text too often.

Each novel/story you write will have its individual items, therefore a checklist for one book may look different in some ways to that for another. You can also amend your table as you go along. For example, you might find that two items really merge into one, for example: showing not telling and showing then telling.

When you have a piece of writing ready for editing, use your table(s).

Note: You may well find that you can check for several things in the one reading: for example, use of beats and subtext in dialogue.

RECOMMENDED BOOKS ON WRITING FICTION

The following are available on Amazon.

Word Power – A guide to creative writing: Julian Birkett, Hollen Street Press Ltd, Slough, Berkshire, 1998.

A basic and digestible beginner's guide to writing, covering characterisation, setting, viewpoint.

How to write a Million: The complete guide to becoming a successful author: Dibell, Scott Card and Turco, Robinson, London, 1999.

Divided into three parts: plot, characterisation and viewpoint, and dialogue. The first two parts are extensive and particularly helpful.

Make a Scene: Crafting a powerful story one scene at a time: Jordan E. Rosenfeld, Writer's Digest Books, Cincinnati, Ohio, 2008.

As its title suggests, covers all aspects of writing a scene: the architecture, core components, different types of scene, with examples given for illustration.

Conflict, Action & Suspense: William Noble, Writer's Digest Books, Cincinnati, Ohio, 1994.

Addresses the 'nuts and bolts' of drama: points of view, use of grammar, dialogue, openings, transitions and endings, to enhance the drama of your story.

Solutions for Writers: Sol Stein, Timelife Editions,

1998.

Covers all basic aspects of writing, including sections on the importance of detail, what affects pace, and techniques for eliminating 'flab'.

Self-Editing for Fiction Writers – How to edit yourself into print: Renni Brown and Dave King, Harper Resource, New York, 2004.

Addresses potential pitfalls such as telling not showing, overuse of exposition, weak dialogue and problems with balance.

On Writing: Stephen King, Hodder and Stoughton, London, 2012.

Part autobiography, part manual, this book provides insightful, useful advice. Helpful for both experienced and beginning writers. Eminently readable and entertaining.

ABOUT THE AUTHOR

Jane Riddell is the author of *Daughters of the Lake*, *Chergui's Child* and *The Bakhtin Chronicles: Academia*. She holds a Masters in Creative Writing.

Jane has an editing business, Choice Words Editing, details of which can be found on her author's website: www.quietfiction.com.

Made in the USA
Charleston, SC
31 January 2017